I AM...

A JOURNAL OF SELF-DISCOVERY

list
doodle
write
color
glue
dream
discover

ISBN-13: 978-1544160917
ISBN-10: 1544160917

design by Laura B. Ginsberg
inspired by pepper and twine via Pinterest

1. MY BEST FEATURES...
2. THINGS I DO WELL...
3. THINGS I HAVE TO WORK HARD AT...
4. THINGS I DON'T LIKE DOING...
5. MOST AWKWARD MOMENTS...
6. FOODS I LIKE...
7. FAVORITE ACTIVITIES...
8. SUPERPOWERS I WISH I HAD...
9. MY GOALS...
10. FAVORITE BIRTHDAYS...
11. FAVORITE FAST FOOD...
12. WHAT I LOVE ABOUT MY ROOM...
13. WHAT I LOVE ABOUT MY LIFE...
14. FAVORITE DESSERTS...
15. WORDS THAT SPEAK TO ME...
16. I WISH I HAD A LIFETIME SUPPLY OF...
17. HARDEST THINGS ABOUT BEING A TEENAGER...
18. FAVORITE SONGS...
19. FAVORITE ARTISTS...
20. FAVORITE BOOKS...
21. FAVORITE MOVIES...
22. FAVORITE TV SHOWS...
23. WHAT I WATCH MOST ON NETFLIX...
24. WHAT I LOVE ABOUT SPRING...
25. WHAT I LOVE ABOUT SUMMER...
26. WHAT I LOVE ABOUT WINTER...
27. WHAT I LOVE ABOUT FALL...
28. FAVORITE WEATHER...
29. FAVORITE DAY...
30. MY LEAST FAVORITE MOVIES...
31. MY LEAST FAVORITE BOOKS...
32. FICTIONAL CHARACTERS I LIKE...
33. FAVORITE HOLIDAY MOVIES...
34. GAMES I PLAYED AS A KID...
35. FOODS I LOVED AS A KID...
36. FAVORITE FAMILY TRADITIONS...
37. WORST MEMORIES FROM CHILDHOOD...
38. MY BIGGEST ARGUMENTS...
39. MY DREAM LIFE...
40. HIGHLIGHTS OF MY LIFE SO FAR...
41. MY STRENGTHS...
42. MY WEAKNESSES...
43. MY GUILTY PLEASURES...
44. MY PET PEEVES...
45. THINGS I WANT TO IMPROVE...
46. CURRENT SHOPPING LIST...
47. THINGS I WANT TO TRY...
48. THINGS I HAVE LOST...
49. FAVORITE SNACKS...
50. THINGS THAT MAKE ME HAPPY...
51. TIMES I GOT IN TROUBLE...
52. I WANT TO LEARN TO...
53. THINGS I WANT TO BE BETTER AT DOING...
54. STRANGE THINGS I'VE EATEN...
55. STRANGE PLACES I'VE BEEN...
56. WAYS I'VE CHANGED...
57. CAKE FLAVORS I'VE HAD...
58. MY PHOBIAS...
59. THINGS I CAN SEE...
60. WHAT I ALWAYS CARRY WITH ME...
61. MY ADDICTIONS...
62. MY CELEBRITY CRUSHES...
63. MY FAVORITE APPS...
64. WAYS I DE-STRESS...
65. THINGS I RECENTLY MADE...
66. THINGS I'VE DESTROYED...
67. PLACES I WANT TO GO...
68. PEOPLE I MOST ADMIRE...
69. THINGS I REMEMBER FROM SCIENCE CLASS...
70. THINGS I REMEMBER FROM MATH CLASS...
71. THINGS I REMEMBER FROM HISTORY CLASS...
72. MY FAVORITE TEACHERS...
73. MY FRIENDS...
74. MY ENEMIES...
75. WHEN I HELPED SOMEONE...
76. WHAT MY FRIENDS SAY ABOUT ME...
77. THINGS THAT MADE ME HAPPY...
78. THINGS THAT MADE ME SAD...
79. FUNNIEST MOMENTS...
80. ON A DESERTED ISLAND I WOULD NEED...
81. BEST ADVICE I EVER GOT...
82. THINGS IN THE WORLD I WANT TO IMPROVE...
83. SONGS THAT CHANGE MY MOOD...
84. MY FIRST MEMORIES...
85. MY DREAM HOME...
86. MY LUCKY CHARM...
87. MOTIVATIONAL QUOTES...
88. THINGS I AM THANKFUL FOR...
89. THINGS I FEAR...
90. NO ONE KNOWS...
91. RAINY DAY ACTIVITIES...
92. FAMILY HISTORY...
93. THINGS I LIKE ABOUT MY FRIENDS...
94. THINGS THAT INSPIRE ME...
95. THINGS THAT CAUSE ME STRESS...
96. THINGS I COLLECT...
97. THINGS I NEED TO THROW AWAY...
98. MY FAILURES...
99. FAVORITE PIZZA TOPPINGS...
100. THINGS I'VE FOUND...
101. WORST HABITS...
102. LIES I'VE TOLD...
103. FAVORITE ANIMALS...
104. I LOVE MY...
105. I AM...

introduction

WHO ARE YOU? It's an important question that everyone gets asked at some point — whether for a college application or in a job interview. WHAT MAKES YOU SPECIAL? WHY DO YOU STAND OUT IN A CROWD? Such difficult questions...and sometimes the hardest part of any journey into ourselves is staring at a blank page. Perhaps you want to write an essay or a book about your life, or maybe you're just trying to figure out some things about yourself, but you're not sure where to start. You might even have beautifully blank journals that you are itching to write in, but you're too worried about messing up the pages. I understand. I've been there too. I've also had many writing students stare at me blankly when I ask them to tell me something about themselves. So, to help them — and you — figure some things out, I've created this journal of self-discovery. Use the prompts to get your journey started. Doodle. Use color. Glue things in it. Write just a few words per page or fill it up to the edges with a short story or reasons why you feel a certain way. The rules are up to you.

Make it yours and have fun!
Laura

MY BEST FEATURES...

THINGS
I DO
WELL...

THINGS I HAVE TO WORK HARD TO AT...

THINGS I DON'T LIKE DOING...

MOST AWKWARD MOMENTS...

FOODS I LIKE...

FAVORITE ACTIVITIES...

SUPER-POWERS I WISH I HAD...

MY GOALS...

FAVORITE BIRTHDAYS...

FAVORITE
FAST FOOD...

WHAT I LOVE ABOUT MY ROOM...

WHAT I LOVE ABOUT MY LIFE...

FAVORITE DESSERTS...

WORDS THAT SPEAK TO ME...

I WISH I HAD A LIFETIME SUPPLY OF...

HARDEST THINGS ABOUT BEING A TEENAGER...

FAVORITE SONGS...

18

FAVORITE ARTISTS...

FAVORITE BOOKS...

FAVORITE MOVIES...

FAVORITE TV SHOWS...

WHAT I WATCH MOST ON NETFLIX...

WHAT I LOVE ABOUT SPRING...

WHAT I LOVE ABOUT SUMMER...

WHAT I LOVE ABOUT WINTER...

WHAT I LOVE ABOUT FALL...

FAVORITE WEATHER...

28

FAVORITE DAY...

MY LEAST FAVORITE MOVIES...

MY LEAST FAVORITE BOOKS...

FICTIONAL CHARACTERS I LIKE...

FAVORITE HOLIDAY MOVIES...

GAMES I PLAYED AS A KID...

FOODS I LOVED AS A KID...

FAVORITE FAMILY TRADITIONS...

WORST MEMORIES FROM CHILDHOOD...

MY BIGGEST ARGUMENTS...

MY DREAM LIFE...

HIGHLIGHTS OF MY LIFE SO FAR...

MY STRENGTHS..

MY WEAKNESSES...

42

MY GUILTY PLEASURES...

MY PET PEEVES...

THINGS I WANT TO IMPROVE...

CURRENT SHOPPING LIST...

THINGS
I WANT
TO TRY...

THINGS I HAVE LOST...

FAVORITE SNACKS...

THINGS THAT MAKE ME HAPPY...

TIMES I GOT IN TROUBLE...

I WANT TO LEARN TO...

THINGS I WANT TO BE BETTER AT DOING...

STRANGE THINGS I'VE EATEN...

STRANGE PLACES I'VE BEEN...

WAYS I'VE CHANGED...

CAKE FLAVORS I'VE HAD...

MY PHOBIAS...

58

THINGS
I CAN
SEE...

59

WHAT I ALWAYS CARRY WITH ME...

60

MY ADDICTIONS...

61

MY
CELEBRITY
CRUSHES...

62

MY FAVORITE APPS...

WAYS I DE-STRESS...

THINGS I RECENTLY MADE...

THINGS I'VE DESTROYED...

PLACES I WANT TO GO...

PEOPLE I MOST ADMIRE...

THINGS I REMEMBER FROM SCIENCE CLASS...

THINGS I REMEMBER FROM MATH CLASS...

THINGS I REMEMBER FROM HISTORY CLASS...

MY FAVORITE TEACHERS...

MY
FRIENDS...

MY ENEMIES...

WHEN I HELPED SOMEONE...

75

WHAT MY FRIENDS SAY ABOUT ME...

THINGS THAT MADE ME HAPPY...

77

THINGS THAT MADE ME SAD...

FUNNIEST MOMENTS...

ON A DESERTED ISLAND I WOULD NEED...

BEST ADVICE I EVER GOT...

THINGS IN THE WORLD I WANT TO IMPROVE...

82

SONGS THAT CHANGE MY MOOD...

MY
FIRST
MEMORIES...

MY DREAM HOME...

MY LUCKY CHARM...

86

MOTIVATIONAL QUOTES....

THINGS I AM THANKFUL FOR...

THINGS I FEAR...

NO ONE KNOWS...

RAINY DAY ACTIVITIES...

FAMILY HISTORY...

THINGS I LIKE ABOUT MY FRIENDS...

THINGS THAT INSPIRE ME...

THINGS THAT CAUSE ME STRESS...

95

THINGS I COLLECT...

THINGS I NEED TO THROW AWAY...

MY
FAILURES...

FAVORITE PIZZA TOPPINGS...

THINGS I'VE FOUND...

100

WORST HABITS...

LIES I'VE TOLD...

FAVORITE ANIMALS...

I LOVE MY...

I AM...

Made in the USA
Columbia, SC
27 March 2019